Guy Stuff:
Dating and Sexuality

CPH®
Concordia Publishing House

Author: Max Murphy

Editor: Mark Sengele

Your comments and suggestions concerning this material are appreciated. Please write the Editor of Youth Materials, Concordia Publishing House, 3558 S. Jefferson Avenue, St. Louis, MO 63118-3968.

This publication is also available in braille and in large type for the visually impaired. Call 1-800-433-3954 or write to Library for the Blind, 1333 S. Kirkwood Rd., St. Louis, MO 63122-7295.

1 2 3 4 5 6 7 8 9 10   11 10 09 08 07 06 05 04 03 02

Contents

Where Are We Coming From? A Note from the Authors

Thank you for choosing this resource from Concordia Publishing House. Dating and sexuality are topics that affect everyone in one way or another. They are also sensitive topics and can be uneasy to talk about. One of the biggest reasons that adults are nervous when talking about dating and sexuality is that they are ashamed of their past. We are no exception. We do not have a perfect history either; none of us does. This book is not altruistic theory. In this book we show you the same principles that God worked in our lives regarding dating and sexuality and now marriage. We believe that this information will be helpful to you in your own unique journey of faith and relationships. The great news is that for those of us in Christ, God does not keep a record of our history. He has forgiven us through the work of Jesus Christ. Please don't let your own past get in the way of hearing God's truths or training up students in the knowledge of God's will and grace. There is no greater responsibility given to us than training up children and youth in the way of the Lord. If it took perfect people to teach, no one would be qualified. It is our prayer that God's Spirit will use this book to assist you in teaching the truth of the Gospel.

In His service,

Max and Beth

An Introduction to Guy Stuff/Girl Stuff

Why This Series?

Congratulations! By picking up this book, you have recognized that young people are living in a world that has confused God's plan for women and men. Scripture clearly tells us that God intended men and women to be different and therefore have different outlooks on life. Rather than ignoring the differences, we have chosen to celebrate them with this study designed specifically for young women or young men. This study explores issues of dating and sexuality.

Using This Study

A variety of settings. The studies in this book parallel each other and, when appropriate, deal with issues or questions unique to girls or guys. Because of this layout, the lessons may be used in a variety of settings including Sunday morning Bible class, a topical youth night, single-gender classes, coed classes with gender breakouts, and single gender or coed retreats. Instructions for the different uses are included later in this section and on page 37.

Lesson preparation. The leader's guide contains complete instructions for leading a single-gender class of guys or girls. A complete set of lessons for either girls or guys can be found in each half of this leader's guide. It is assumed that the leader will provide basic classroom supplies including pens and pencils; a chalkboard, whiteboard, or newsprint and markers; and Bibles. Supplies needed for specific lessons are noted on the lesson outline. The leader should make copies of the appropriate student pages for each lesson in quantities sufficient for the number of students in attendance.

Each lesson is outlined for a 60-minute class period. The bonus sections in each lesson can be used to extend that lesson for a longer time period. You should plan to use the optional activities that best meet the needs of your setting and students. If your youth Bible class only gets 40 minutes of real study time, find a good place to break off and then share a Gospel summary pointing to Christ and His love and forgiveness toward sinners. Conclude the session with prayer and pick it up next week.

While the book is designed for use in single gender classes, it may by used for a coed class. In order to teach a coed class, it is necessary to use portions of both the girl and the guy lesson outlines from each side of this book. Sections that should be treated as gender-specific breakouts while working with a coed group are designated with a special symbol. In addition, special suggestions for use with coed groups are available from the Concordia Publishing House Web site. See the center page of this book for more information.

Relationship building. Within each lesson we suggest activities that work well in the whole group and in breakout sections. Whole-group experiences are intended for all students involved. Breakout groups are designed for groups of three to five students to work together. If your total group is small, you may wish to ignore breakout suggestions. If you are teaching in a coed setting, breakout groups can be designed as gender-specific activities.

In an ideal setting, the leader of a gender-specific class should be the same gender as the class. If you are leading a coed group and using gender-specific breakout groups, it would be helpful to have an adult leader of the same gender as each of the breakout groups. It may also be beneficial, however, to have a member of the opposite sex be interviewed or asked to share his or her perspectives at some point for each separate gender cluster.

Supplemental material. Additional resources are available for use with this study. These resources include retreat information, additional activities, clip art, and promotional materials. Also included are supplemental activities for use in coed studies. The resources are available as a free bonus for users of this study at the Concordia Publishing House Web site. See the center page for complete details on how to locate these materials.

THE PERFECT DATE 1

Purpose

Every young man wants to know he is important and respected by others. While family members play an important role in an adolescent's life, a young man will eventually look beyond the family for someone else. There may be many reasons why you want to date. God created male and female with a desire for each other that is still present, even though it has been drastically altered after the fall into sin. Personal desires for acceptance and peer pressure can lead guys into dating. But before we can analyze dating, we must ask, what *is* dating anyway? Is it a rite of passage? Is it just a pastime? Is it an innate drive? Confusion about the purpose of dating may lead some guys to have unreal expectations as to what is involved in a date. Because the first experience sets the pattern for what follows, guys should know from the start what God's will is for their dating life. Often there is no Dating 101 class for them to learn what to do and how to act. This study addresses some of the issues from that kind of class.

Gospel Emphasis

God in His love desires to have a relationship with each one of us and for that reason sent Jesus to make that relationship possible. Christ died for all of us, regardless of how we look or how funny we act sometimes.

Lesson Outline

Activity	Time Suggested	Materials Needed
Dating Game	15 minutes	newsprint with topic list
Speak Your Mind (optional activity)	10 minutes	bag of topics
What about Me?	15 minutes	Guys Student Page 1A
Pyramid Production (optional activity)	15 minutes	see instructions
Song of Songs	20 minutes	Guys Student Page 1B
The Perfect Date	10 minutes	newsprint, markers
Closing	2 minutes	none

Dating Game (15 minutes)

This activity is designed to get guys thinking about how to identify a good date. This will be very effective if you have a group that likes to share stories. List on newsprint or a board the topics listed below:
Having the courage to ask her out
>Meeting her parents
>Deciding what to do
>Determining who pays
>Dealing with curfews
>Saying goodbyes
>Deciding where to go
>Daring to give the first kiss

Use these topics to discuss what goes into a date or to describe the perfect date. Ask students to discuss dates they have been on or heard about. (Caution students to avoid gossip.) What went well? What didn't work? What can they learn from these past experiences? What is their ideal in each of these areas? Try to draw some conclusions about what makes good or bad dates. Example: Good dates give you the opportunity to talk and get to know each other. Bad dates are where you can't talk (for instance, at movies or dances). There is more to a date than "hooking up."

Speak Your Mind—Optional Activity (10 minutes)

Fill a paper bag with paper slips or note cards with topics from the "Dating Game" activity. You may add your own topics if you like. Invite one student at a time to come up and select a topic from the bag. Students must then give a 60-second impromptu speech about their topic. Speeches may include do's and don'ts, other advice, or past history. After the speeches, discuss any new insights and get reactions.

What about Me? (15 minutes)

Ever been to a potluck? Lots of people bring lots of different foods, and everybody goes back for lots of seconds of the things they liked. Let's face it: dating other people can be a little like a potluck. Different people increase our exposure to different things. Being open to new things is a fun part of dating. Who knows? After trying a new activity, hobby, music, or food, you may decide that you think it's great or you "kinda" like it or you can barely stand it or you HATE it!

But some things are part of who we are and should not be compromised—things like VALUES and GOALS. Through our Baptism we gain a baptismal identity. God makes us His very children, and as a result we share values that are different from the world's values. As Christians our values and goals are shaped by our Christian faith.

This activity is designed to encourage guys to more deeply develop an idea about who they are and what they value. This very important process serves as a foundation for decisions they will make in current or future relationships. Identifying core values, goals, and beliefs will help a young man to see himself as God does—as His baptized, redeemed child.

The topic of date rape may come up in the discussion. It is suggested that you research this and other topics beforehand to support you in giving answers to tough questions. Resources to facilitate discussion concerning rape and other critical issues include *The Why Files: When Can I Start Dating? Questions about Love, Sex, and a Cure for Zits* (CPH: 2000) and *Love, Sex, and God* (CPH: 1998).

Recognizing this fact allows young men to seek a partner who shares common values, to set boundaries for sexual activity, and to more easily reject cheap substitutes for real love. Guys' expectations of who they should be is often influenced by their peers, friends, or even the media. This activity will help guys to see what God has made them to be in Holy Baptism. Underscore the fact that we are unique and extremely valuable in God's eyes. Remind them that their goals and values can reflect God's will for all believers (Matthew 10:29–31).

Hand out copies of Guys Student Page 1A. Say, "A once-popular country song states, 'You've got to stand for something, or you'll fall for anything.' Why do you think it might be important to clarify your values before you start dating?" Guide the responses toward the conclusions listed above. Have the guys break into small groups to answer the questions on the student page and then share within their group. After breakout groups have shared, ask for some responses to be shared with the larger group.

Once the students have finished the five-year goals, say, "All that we have is a gift from God! He has also blessed you with a great potential future! We are to take care of all His gifts to us, including our sexuality. It is one of the most powerful gifts God has given to us. With this in mind, how can you best use the gift of sexuality over the next five years? How about over a lifetime?"

> This activity is designed to help your students better understand the factors that influence the choices they make. You may want to incorporate a personality inventory into this activity just to help students begin to think about how each person has different strengths, interests, and abilities.

Pyramid Production—Optional Activity (15 minutes)

Preparation: Assemble "building" materials beforehand such as canned goods, empty (but clean) food containers, small toys, fruit, and so on. Your goal is to select items in different forms, weights, and sizes. Use your imagination and creatively arrange the junk-on-hand.

Divide the class into groups of two to four people. Give groups five minutes to construct a pyramid that has five or more levels. The goal is to create a structure that is as tall and strong as possible using at least five different building materials. After five minutes have passed, let each group evaluate their structure on both strength and height using a 1–10 scale (1=weakest, smallest; 10=sturdiest, tallest). Follow up by discussing these questions: Which building material was most important for your pyramid to achieve it's maximum height and strength? How might this task have been different without a solid base? What purpose does a good foundation have? (Provides stability for everything built upon it.)

After allowing for discussion, read the parable of the wise and foolish builders found in Luke 6:47–49. Say, "A solid foundation is necessary for any building project. The foundation of a strong, secure relationship with others begins with a strong relationship with God in Christ. We love because He first loved us. The most healthy relationships also rise above our own sins and needs, rooted in God's forgiveness and built upon who God made you to be. God started laying that foundation by identifying goals and shaping your values as His precious child. A combination of time, loyalty, and communication builds intimacy and security in relationships with God and others."

Song of Songs (20 minutes)

Distribute copies of Guys Student Page 1B to each student. This study highlights God's intimate relationship with us and encourages guys to prepare for a future exclusive relationship by practicing the same concepts in their social relationships.

Dating takes time and does not produce an instant relationship. As teens begin dating, they are influenced by how others perceive them. Teens need to be reminded the truth that who they are in Christ greatly impacts or determines what they do. Personal identity is a powerful factor in dating. How much more so is the new identity our Lord gives us when He adopts us as His very own family and declares us righteous.

The intimacy and security in a strong relationship need some TLC in order to grow: time, loyalty, and communication. God's plan for this kind of intimacy in a marriage relationship is shown in the example of the beloved and the lover in the Song of Songs (Song of Solomon). Developing and managing TLC in an exclusive relationship can be a lot of work. As sinners, we are unable to manage on our own. It is only in Christ that all relationships are restored and made perfect. Teens can learn aspects of intimacy as they practice applying these concepts in their social relationships and early, less-committed dating relationships.

Have the students study each of the Bible passages listed on the student page. Each verse gives an example of time, loyalty, or communication. Encourage the group to relate the verses to the given topic. Have them record their answers on the student page and share them with the group. Once students have shared their answers, read or summarize the explanation for each section below:

Some Thoughts Concerning Relationships

Time

Song of Songs 2:10–13; 7:11–12. It would be hard to say that you have a close relationship with a person you never spend time with. A relationship is built over time by exploring common interests, getting to know a person's likes and dislikes, and observing how that person acts in social situations.

Do you think the saying "Quality, not quantity" is true concerning time spent in relationships? Why or why not? (Both quality and quantity of time are needed for a growing relationship.) In fact, it may take lots of time (a great quantity) to achieve some good quality time.

Loyalty

Song of Songs 1:5–6. Loyalty means acting with truthfulness and not betraying another's trust. Often dating relationships contain partial truths, outright lies, exaggerated stories, or false claims because people are afraid to reveal who they really are. The beloved here does not try to puff herself up to be something she is not. She admits her shortcomings and does not paint a false picture. In spite of the risk, she is still adored by friends and her lover. Each individual is known completely by God. God intentionally made each of us different for His purpose, and we must not be afraid to let someone know how unique we really are. A strong relationship built on loyalty begins with honesty, integrity, and trustworthiness.

What potential problems in a relationship might be avoided by acting in truth and honesty with respect to who God made you to be? (Answers will vary.)

Communication

Song of Songs 1:15–16. The Book of Song of Songs is a dialogue between the beloved and the lover (with side comments from friends), which illustrates the importance of conversation in building a relationship. Conversation that builds intimacy should probe beneath a person's obvious likes and dislikes, exploring personal goals, spiritual maturity, and values.

Getting girls to open up about personal values and beliefs can be a challenge. No one may feel comfortable at first, until some initial foundation stones can be laid. What can you do to make it easier? (Possible answers: be an active listener, be willing to share first.)

Some Thoughts Concerning God's Relationship with Us

Now look at each of the corresponding verses and themes as they relate to our faith life. God wants relationships between His people to reflect His relationship with us through Jesus Christ, His Son. The Bible says that Christ is the groom and the church is His bride. We have a great example in Christ of what it means for a man to love his wife. The following verses will show how God has displayed TLC to us. How is the theme demonstrated in each verse?

Time

Psalm 16:11; 84:10. God is not bound by time like we are. His desire isn't that we just spend some quality time with Him, but He desires for us to be in His presence for all eternity. Jesus' mission on earth made that a reality for us. In the meantime, the best way to experience His intimate love occurs when the Holy Spirit works in you as you spend time in His Word, in prayer, in worship, in Communion, and by living out His grace that first came in your Baptism.

How has God given quality time or quantity of time in developing a relationship with us, His people? (Both quality and quantity come through worship, Scripture, and other significant life/faith experiences.)

Loyalty

Psalm 32:5. The strength of a relationship can be directly correlated to the level of loyalty and truth between people in that relationship. God works in our lives, helping us to be open and honest with Him (He already knows everything about us) in a way that clears away the garbage of sin between us. When we truthfully acknowledge our standing before God, we see that we don't belong in His presence. Remember the beloved's rating of her own beauty? We, too, see our ugliness of sin. The great news is that God puts us in a new standing before Him by the work of Jesus Christ and says, "I love you and want to be with you," and we can now see our standing before Him in a new light. God sees the beauty of Christ reflected in us. And this Gospel truth must be lived out in our lives—for example, in how we treat others in a dating relationship.

What does God's loyalty mean to you? (Answers will vary.)

Communication

Jeremiah 29:11–13; 1 Thessalonians 5:17. God has in mind the perfect plan for your life, including your dating life. Do you know what it is? We know that His plan is for you to have a relationship with Him in this life and throughout eternity. Other details unfold over time as He guides our lives through faith. Talk to Him. Tell Him what's on your mind. Share your "what ifs?" and your "what nows?" His unchanging, eternal promise is that He will be found by you and will hear your prayers. He guides your faith and works through His Word to direct your decisions, lifestyle choices, and directions.

In what other ways does God communicate with us? (Scripture shows a past, present, and future glimpse of God's great love for you. In Baptism God says, "You are My child." Through Holy Communion God says, "You are My honored guest. I forgive you and will strengthen you.")

The Perfect Date (10 minutes)

Often expectations for dates are set so high that anything may seem to fall short. This activity will help guys evaluate what is important in a date and how to accomplish it. You will need newsprint and markers. Use this as a brainstorming session. On one side write "Goals" and on the other side write "Plans."

First discuss the purpose of dating and put these thoughts under "Goals." Tell the students to think about what they want to accomplish. Is the purpose of a date to get to know another person, to have fun, to avoid loneliness, to feel macho, or . . . what? Because males have a strong sex drive, a popular sinful goal of dating may be to "score" or get involved in some kind of sexual activity. Guys may even be asked, "How far did you get?" This only shows that some people's goals for dating can be different from God's plan. Point out that goals should demonstrate a respect for God, others, and self. Once you have some goals written down, start asking for ways to accomplish those goals and list them under "Plans." You should begin to develop a pretty good selection of dating ideas. Tell the group that the perfect date would be one where God's work is evident and His name is praised through us and our behavior.

Closing (2 minutes)

Close this session with the following prayer: "Heavenly Father, Your love for us cannot be matched. Forgive us for not loving You or others like You loved us. We thank You for accepting us as we are and desiring and empowering the best in all we do. May Your Spirit live in our lives that we may continue to develop the connection You have made with us. Through Your Son, Jesus Christ, we pray. Amen."

What about Me?

How would you describe yourself to an Internet chat-room friend?

What is your favorite characteristic about yourself?

List your strengths, interests, and abilities. What don't you like to do?

In each of the categories listed below, list two goals you want to accomplish in the next five years.

Personal Life:

    Academic

    Career

    Relationships

Spiritual Life:

    Prayer

    Bible Study

    Worship

    Lifestyle

For what areas of your sexuality do you most thank God? For what do you want His help in the area of your sexuality over the next five years? During your lifetime? How might your attitudes and actions expressing your sexuality during the next five years affect the rest of your life?

Some Thoughts Concerning Relationships

Time, loyalty, and communication are needed in developing and maintaining a good relationship. We can see from the Song of Songs that all of these elements are present. The lover is the male in this poem. Notice the time, loyalty, and communication shown by the man in this story. He is a great example of what we as guys should be for our girlfriends and wives.

Look at each of the corresponding themes and verses. How is the theme demonstrated in each verse?

Time
Song of Songs 2:10–13; 7:11–12
Do you think the saying "Quality, not quantity" is true concerning time spent in relationships? Why or why not?

Loyalty
Song of Songs 1:5–6
What potential relationship problems might be avoided by acting in truth and honesty with respect to who God made you to be?

Communication
Song of Songs 1:15–16
Getting someone to open up about personal things like values and beliefs can be a challenge. What can you do to make it easier?

Now look back over your answers and each theme. How do you feel about these characteristics, and do you think they are important? Why?

Some Thoughts Concerning God's Relationship with Us

Now look at each of the corresponding verses and themes as they relate to our faith life. God wants relationships between people to be modeled after His relationship with us through Jesus Christ, His Son. The Bible says that Christ is the groom and the church is His bride. We have a great example in Christ of what it means for a man to love his wife.

The following verses will show how God has displayed TLC to us. How is the theme demonstrated in each verse?

Time
Psalm 16:11; 84:10
How has God given quality time or quantity of time in developing a relationship with us, His people?

Loyalty
Psalm 32:5
What does God's loyalty mean to you?

Communication
Jeremiah 29:11–13; 1 Thessalonians 5:17
In what other ways does God communicate with us?

Looking back at these answers, we see that God has been gracious throughout human history, extending also to us. In response to His love and filled with His Spirit, we can show TLC to those around us. How can you demonstrate TLC in the relationships in your life?

A Perfect Love 2

Purpose

Many young men are interested in developing a relationship with a girl. They want to be accepted and liked for who they are and be "successful" with girls. Guys can be very competitive. Having a relationship with a girl builds self-confidence and can aid in social acceptance. However, many guys lack the knowledge about what makes a healthy relationship. There is a shortage of healthy relationships in the world for them to learn from. Even biblical characters provide a picture of fallen man in a struggle to relate. Only God demonstrates a perfect example of divine love and the nature of a healthy relationship with others.

Gospel Emphasis

We have the perfect heavenly Father, who loves unconditionally. Living in His love in Christ, we are enabled to feel good about who we are as God's creatures, forgiven and given unique gifts, talents, and abilities. God's love makes it possible for us to make God-pleasing decisions concerning our relationships. The more we respect ourselves and others as God's children, the more respectfully we will relate to others.

Lesson Outline

Activity	Time Suggested	Materials Needed
Either/Or (optional activity)	10 minutes	marker board or newsprint
What's in a Friend?	15 minutes	newsprint, markers
Love Is—Part 1	15 minutes	Guys Student Page 2A
Examples of Love	10 minutes	none
Love Is—Part 2	20 minutes	Guys Student Page 2B
Closing	2 minutes	none

Either/Or—Optional Activity (10 minutes)

This activity is designed to get guys thinking and talking about the qualities they look for when making a friend. It is also intended to help guys to discover that many of the same characteristics found in a good male friend are also important for a good relationship with a girl. Most guys don't talk as much as girls do about friends and friendship. Encourage guys to open up as much as possible. Try to create a "safe" place for students to share their thoughts. This may be done by modeling such behavior yourself. You may want to describe a close friend you have and why this person is your friend.

List on newsprint or a marker board the qualities given below. You may want to reveal only one choice at a time. Have students move to one side of the room or the other depending upon their response to the question "Which of these two characteristics is most important as you look for a friend?" Ask students to give reasons for their choice. Once you have completed all four choice pairs, ask the question "What qualities do you think God looks for in people?"

• creativity or humor?
• looks or personality?
• popularity or generosity?
• hygiene or thoughtfulness?

What's in a Friend? (15 minutes)

This activity is designed to show guys how important it is to have relationships with girls who are also friends. Despite what some guys think, the word *girlfriend* is NOT an oxymoron. Some of the best relationships occur when you have a genuine friendship before it becomes romantic. A guy should learn to respect his girlfriend enough to treat her as a true friend. It means giving yourself to the friendship, not just trying to get something out of it. It also means spending time together even when there is no possibility of physical/sexual activity.

Divide students into small groups. Provide each group a sheet of newsprint and markers. Say, "Your assignment is to create two lists of characteristics. One list should describe your best friend. The other list should describe your ideal girlfriend. Try to rank the characteristics in order of importance." Give guys seven or eight minutes to develop their lists. Invite the groups back together to share their lists. Ask, "Where do the qualities you listed differ between a friend and a girlfriend? Where are they similar? Why do you think it might be important to have a girlfriend who is a friend as well?"

Love Is—Part 1 (15 minutes)

Distribute copies of Guys Student Page 2A. Read together 1 Corinthians 13:1–8a. Allow students time to answer the questions on the student page. Guide a discussion of their findings following these suggestions:

Whom is the apostle Paul speaking of in this passage?
(Christ)
How has this been expressed?
(In Christ's keeping the Law on our behalf and His selfless sacrifice upon the cross for our sake.)
How do you receive this love in order to reflect it to others?
(This love is given solely by God's grace and forgiveness given in our Baptism.)
How might people express their love for someone?
(Answers will vary. The text suggests through words, personal characteristics, and the giving of gifts.)

What have you done to show someone that you love them?
(Answers will vary.)

What would you say is the main point of verses 1 to 3?

(We may have a variety of gifts and talents, but they don't mean much if we don't use them sincerely in love for others. In this way love is one of the most important things we can possess.)

List the seven things that describe what love is and the nine things that love is not.

(Love is patient, kind, joyful in truth, protecting, trusting, hopeful, and persevering. Love is not envious, boastful, proud, rude, self-seeking, easily angered, interested in keeping a record of wrongs, delighting in evil, and capable of failing.)

How do these compare with your relationships and those you have seen involving others?

(Answers will vary. Go down the list if the group is having difficulty.)

Examples of Love (10 minutes)

Ask each student to think of a person who demonstrates the best example of love. Make sure that each student has a definite person in mind before you divide the students into pairs and have each student tell his partner about the loving person he chose to describe. After five minutes or so, go around the room and have each person share as much about his loving example as he feels comfortable sharing.

Say, "We all have loving people who touch our lives, but not as many as we should. Many people love with selfish attitudes and actions. Sinful people can never give perfect love. There is only One who has ever done that, Jesus Christ. God gives us the picture of perfect love in His Word. His perfect love is *agape*, a completely selfless and giving love that only seeks good for the receiver. In studying 1 Corinthians 13, we see that Jesus fulfills the description of love perfectly."

Love Is—Part 2 (20 minutes)

Hand out copies of Guys Student Page 2B to each student. Allow students time to work together in small groups to study how Christ fulfilled each characteristic of love listed in 1 Corinthians 13. After allowing time for groups to study, use these notes to lead a discussion with the whole group. Remember to point out at each example that Jesus is much more than a role model who fulfills the Law for us. He is perfect love, and He lived in perfect love for us. He forgives our failure to live up to these characteristics. He also helps us to grow and better live in His perfect love with others.

Love Is Patient

Instant gratification is a part of our culture. From modems to McDonald's, things just aren't fast enough to satisfy us. Guys sometimes want to immediately become physically involved in ways that are reserved for married couples. Being patient often means setting our own needs aside to wait for a greater good. Jesus understood this—in Matthew 4:1–4, He could have instantly satisfied His hunger pangs by giving in to Satan's temptation. The salvation of the entire world depended on His living a life without sin. For God's greater good, Jesus waited for His needs to be filled in the Father's time.

How might patience lead to a greater good in a love relationship? (God promises to bless those who wait on His timing and plans for a relationship.)

Love Is Kind

Have you experienced any unexplainable "random acts of kindness"? Whether you have been the giver or the receiver, you might have experienced some benefit. In a recent popular movie the main character does a favor for three different people without expecting a favor in return. These people are moved by this act of kindness, and instead of paying the favor back, they "pay it forward" to three others in need—beginning a chain reaction.

True love is not only a feeling; it's also an action. God's kind of love is sensitive to the needs of guys and girls. He acts through the kind of love that Jesus shows us in Matthew 14:14.

Why are acts of kindness so powerful? How might kindness transform a relationship? (An act of kindness can soften the hardest heart. It provides an opportunity for the believer to share the Gospel with those who are being served.)

Love Is Humble

Humility is not even close to the top of the list of the desired characteristics for most high school guys. There are only two adjectives that Jesus uses to describe Himself in the New Testament. They both occur in Matthew 11:29. Imagine a king who trades his crown for street clothes and who goes to the impoverished parts of town to provide all-you-can-eat buffets for the people. Imagine that he sits down in the street to eat and talk with them. He is highly educated, but speaks simply so the common people will understand about his justice and mercy, his laws and love. He knows his own worth, his value, and yet he gives every single person his attention as if he were speaking to his most highly honored guest. There is no envy, boastfulness, or pride. There is only love. The disciple John speaks of Jesus in this way in John 13:3–5, 12–17.

Why is humility so hard for most guys to express? What does the world think of humbleness? (Because of our sinful nature, humility is difficult for most guys. The world views humility as a sign of weakness, yet Christ shows true strength in His humility.)

Love Is Selfless

Often our sinful nature causes us to become selfish in our relationships. This is encouraged when guys ask each other, "What did you get from her?" or other similar questions. Guys often want to know what's in a relationship for them. Thankfully God has given up His all for us. He set the example of a selfless and giving love. We can only give to Him out of what He has given to us. Jesus gave up everything, even His life, for our salvation. In Romans 5:7–8 we are reminded that Christ died for us, in spite of who we are, while we are still sinners. He received nothing in return for His act of selflessness. We can demonstrate that love to those around us as the Holy Spirit strengthens us for service.

What do you think a relationship would be like if both people involved were completely selfless? (While our sinful nature makes this impossible, relationships that include selfless love for each other are often very strong.)

Love Is Forgiving and Encouraging

Relationships are ruined by offenses that are never forgotten. Families may have members that have not spoken for years because of an argument that was never resolved. Put-downs and pointed fingers can also keep intimacy from growing. When forgiveness and encouragement abound, there can be healthy growth in relationships, even in tough times. It is best when we can continue to have a friendly relationship with a girl whom we once dated. When we treat others respectfully, we have a better chance of relationships ending peacefully, even when there is pain. God in His mercy has not held back His forgiveness and encouragement from us, although we are entirely at fault. In John 8:2–11, Jesus would have had the authority to condemn the woman caught in adultery for her offense, and yet He forgave her. We sin greatly; we are also greatly forgiven and encouraged to live in the light of His love. By God's grace we won't take His forgiveness for granted and lose our desire to try to live for Him. 1 Thessalonians 3:11–13 reminds us of how much God desires to bless us.

How does this truth encourage us each day? (We know that Jesus forgives each time we need it. By His grace, He continues to shower us with His love.)

Love Is Forever

Can anything last forever? Our culture is marked by short-lived and disposable things: pre-made meals, single-use disposable cameras, seasonal fashions, and changing fads. This trend is also seen in relationships, as many marriages end in divorce. If love is conditional, once the affection and feelings wear off, there is little need for the partner anymore. Thanks be to God that His love for us is without condition, bound by His unbreakable promise or covenant. Jesus' last words to His bride, the church, tenderly reflect this perfect love in Matthew 28:20.

How does it feel to know that God will always love you perfectly and completely? How might this strengthen you in a relationship? How might it encourage you when you are not in a relationship? (Knowing that we are perfectly loved empowers us to share this love with others. It also reminds us that even if we aren't in a relationship with another person, we are still greatly loved.)

Closing (2 minutes)

Close this session with the following prayer: "Heavenly Father, You have developed a perfect relationship with us in Jesus Christ. We confess that we often look other places to find relationships before we look to You. Lord, thank You for calling us by name and making us Yours in Baptism. Remind us daily of this relationship, and guide us in our interactions with those around us. In Jesus' name we pray. Amen."

Love Is—Part 1
Read 1 Corinthians 13:1–8a.

Whom is the apostle Paul speaking of in this passage?

How has this been expressed?

How do we receive this love in order to reflect it to others?

How might people express their love for someone?

What have you done to show someone that you love them?

What would you say is the main point of verses 1 to 3?

List the seven things that describe what love is and the nine things that love is not.

How do these compare with your relationships and those you have seen involving others?

Love Is—Part 2

We have a God who is Love. He is the perfect fulfillment of 1 Corinthians 13. Look at these examples of how Jesus showed perfect love throughout His earthly ministry. Read the selected verses and describe how Jesus fulfilled each characteristic of love.

Love Is Patient • Matthew 4:1–11
How might patience lead to a greater good in a love relationship?

Love Is Kind • Matthew 14:14
Why are acts of kindness so powerful? How might kindness transform a relationship?

Love Is Humble • Matthew 11:29; John 13:3–5, 12–17
Why is humility so hard for most guys to express? What does the world think of humbleness?

Love Is Selfless • Romans 5:7–8; John 15:13
What do you think a relationship would be like if both people involved were completely selfless?

Love Is Forgiving and Encouraging • John 8:2–11; 1 Thessalonians 3:11–13
How does this truth encourage us each day?

Love Is Forever • Matthew 28:20
How does it feel to know that God will always love you perfectly and completely? How might this strengthen you in a relationship? How might it encourage you when you are not in a relationship?

3 Just Do It?

Purpose

In a "just do it" culture that targets teens, guys are pressured to be *men* by having sex. Because of the nonchalant attitude our society holds toward premarital sex, guys who do not claim to be sexually active are open to ridicule and misunderstanding. In reality, there is much more to lose than to gain by becoming sexually active. The reality is that young men will not gain lasting or fulfilling respect or importance by becoming sexually active. Premarital sex usually lowers self-respect, increases fear and insecurity, and reduces a guy's feeling of value and importance. Sex was designed by God as an expression of covenant love, a love that mirrors His love for us.

Gospel Emphasis

God wants only the best for His children. He loves us so much that He tells us what is going to be best for us as sexual beings. He promises never to allow us to be tempted beyond what we can bear, and He forgives us when we are weak.

Lesson Outline

Activity	Time Suggested	Materials Needed
TLC Toss	15 minutes	tennis ball, alarm clock, phone receiver, journal, precious object
Paying the Price	15 minutes	Guys Student Page 3A
Making a Level Table	15 minutes	newsprint/board, small table (optional)
How Far Can I Go?	15 minutes	newsprint/board
10 Rotten Reasons (optional activity)	10 minutes	Guys Student Page 3B
Closing	2 minutes	none

TLC Toss (15 minutes)

This activity is designed to reinforce the idea that relationships take TLC (time, loyalty, and communication). It will demonstrate that trying to "juggle" all of the elements of a relationship can be harder than it seems. Relationships take work and practice. They get even tougher when you add physical touch and contact to the equation. You will need the four items listed below. A deeper explanation of each item also follows.

Form groups of six to eight people and have them sit or stand in a circle, allowing for some elbow room. Tell the groups they will be tossing an object to other group members across from them following these guidelines: Objects may not be tossed to a person more than once until everyone has had a turn. Students will always toss the object to the same person. The leader should help establish the pattern. You may want to practice with a tennis ball until groups get the hang of the pattern. The game becomes more difficult as additional objects (from the list below) are added and used simultaneously.

Order	Object	Represents
first	alarm clock	time
second	journal	loyalty
third	phone receiver	communication
fourth	precious object*	touch

* Choose something fragile with sentimental attachment, such as an heirloom. Don't worry! This object will not actually be thrown into the rotation, but will serve as a catalyst for the discussion.

As each item is tossed into the rotation, review these intimacy-building concepts:

Time (alarm clock)

A relationship begins by spending meaningful time with someone. This does not include time spent touching or kissing. An activity that allows you to explore common interests, to get to know a girl's likes and dislikes, or to see how she acts in social situations is time well spent.

Loyalty (journal)

Loyalty means to remain committed to something or someone. It involves keeping someone's trust. In a relationship you need to be open and share personal thoughts, opinions, and feelings—gently and truthfully, as you would do in a journal. Too often guys in a relationship feel the need to put up a false front in order to be accepted. In reality, by trying to fit in, we may blend in so well we aren't noticed or appreciated as individuals. We need not be afraid to let others know how unique, amazing, and even complex God has made us. Each person is an individual who is completely known and loved by God. The foundation for a strong relationship is built with loyalty. The journal symbolizes loyalty and trust between people.

Communication (phone receiver)

Talking and listening play an important part in getting to know someone. Conversation that builds intimacy probes beneath the obvious likes and dislikes of a person and explores their personal goals, reveals their level of spiritual maturity, and presents their value system. It takes time to achieve this!

Touch (precious object)

We've learned that a relationship takes TLC. But once a relationship progresses, it starts to involve a fourth element, touch. For some guys, this may be seen as the only important element of a relationship with a girl. God has a different plan. Along with time, loyalty, and communication, touch is an important part of a relationship. Touch also potentially has great consequences.

Touch is an important part of a relationship, but if it is misused, it can also diminish or destroy a couple's intimacy. Like this valuable heirloom, God made our sexuality unique and precious. Because it involves and impacts one's entire body, soul, heart, and mind, it needs to be handled so carefully that it is not damaged. God's intention is that full, intimate touch be handled with awe and respect only within the realm of total commitment—marriage. Guys are dealing with an extremely valuable individual, loved by God. It is not right to be careless with a treasure. It is not right to become sexually active with a girl until marriage. God has given men the responsibility to show integrity and values as they relate with women.

Paying the Price (15 minutes)

Distribute copies of Guys Student Page 3A. Encourage students to read and study 1 Corinthians 6:18–20 and respond to the questions in small groups. After allowing time for groups to work, discuss the findings with the whole group.

Why is sex apart from marriage idolatry?

(Sexual activity outside of the bonds of marriage is sin. Sin displaces God in our lives and makes sex idolatrous.)

How is sexual sin different from other sins?

(Sexual sin is against the body, which is a temple of God that is miraculously able to become one with another person through sexual intercourse. Becoming one is not to be taken lightly—a breakup can leave both lives emotionally shattered.)

Why do you think this is so?

(Answers will vary; see the answer above.)

Do you agree?

(Answers will vary.)

What is both exciting and scary about verse 19?

(The fact that God dwells inside of us can convict us, but also can provide a source of great strength and encouragement.)

How would you define *temple* in this context?

(Answers will vary. A place where God chooses to dwell.)

Why can we not do whatever we want with our body?

(It is not ours; we were bought with a price.)

What was the price paid for us?

(Jesus' life given on the cross—see 1 Peter 1:18–19.)

If you really believe this text, how might you respond?

(With guilty conviction because of our sin, but in joyful freedom in the forgiveness of God.)

For Further Discussion
In what ways might sexuality be handled carelessly by a guy or girl? (Sexual involvement begins too quickly and progresses too far, not requiring a trust-and-commitment level, taking a risk that sounds fun. Answers may vary.)
What might be a definition of total commitment outside marriage? (None. Saying, "But we love each other," getting engaged, or living together to determine compatibility are typically used to rationalize sexual intimacy.
All these reasons fall short of the commitment in a covenant relationship that God intended us to experience; sexual relations outside of marriage is idolatry.)

Making a Level Table (15 minutes)

On newsprint or a marker board draw a picture of a table, showing all four legs. On each leg write one of the following: *commitment*, *communication*, *time*, and *physical contact*. Talk about how a level table is balanced, with each leg of the table being as long as the others. A healthy relationship should be similarly balanced. Physical contact can be extended fully only when commitment is also extended fully. God has established that full commitment exists only in marriage, and full physical expression through sexual intercourse should wait until then. When any component of a relationship is extended farther than the level of commitment, there are negative effects emotionally, physically, and spiritually. God wired us that way. Explore some possible problems that might occur if a relationship doesn't have the proper balance. Talk about how to prevent these problems. Encourage guys to see that they can hardly have a full commitment to a relationship during their high school years, which means that other aspects of the relationship need to be held back as well. Even engagement is not a full commitment; engagements are often broken.

How Far Can I Go? (15 minutes)

Ironically, this question is sometimes asked after teens have already stepped over the line they had established in their conscience. Our conscience is a God-given gift that can guide us to make and stick with God-pleasing decisions. However, even our conscience feels the effects of sin. Sometimes our mind works hard to rationalize sin and ignore the alarm bells of a guilty conscience. When we rationalize sin, it chips away at our conscience's ability to steer us to make wise decisions. Proverbs 7:1–3 reminds us that our conscience is strengthened through the study of God's Word.

Help guys to acknowledge that there are absolute truths about sexuality that God has given us. See if they can build a list, which it may be helpful to keep posted in the room and add to as needed. The principles might include the following: Sex is God's idea (Genesis 1:28). Sex is good (Genesis 1:31). Sex is intended for use in a covenant relationship (Genesis 1:24). Sex is more than just a physical act (Matthew 5:27–28). Sex is NOT designed for members within the same family, for same-sex partners, or for humans with animals (Leviticus 18). (Students may be able to think of additional ways in which sinful flesh perverts the divine gift of sexuality.)

Not every sexual issue is black and white. Students have questions about sex not because they haven't been given enough information, but because they experience the tension of conflicting values in our society. You need to be prepared if they ask, "Am I still a virgin if I give or receive oral sex?" "Isn't penetration of the penis into the vagina the proper definition of having sex?" or "God doesn't say it's wrong, so why do I feel guilty?" The following insights may be helpful in answering these types of questions:

Touch is a natural expression of our affection for those around us, and it is possible to touch in ways that are nonsexual yet loving. Certain types of nonsexual touching are a product of investing significant time, loyalty, and communication in a relationship, and convey awe and respect for a person.

However, there are actions that cross the line from affection into passionate expression. This line should be guarded with preestablished boundaries, prayer, and a partner who shares your Christian faith and with whom you share common ideals. But this can be difficult. Guys want to know that they are appreciated and have the approval of their partner. Guys know that girls want the attention and affection that touch brings. But a girl's desire for attention and affection can too often be taken advantage of by an aggressive guy. A girl may give sex to feel loved and secure. A guy may say words pledging love and commitment just to get sex. Both are dangerous. Touch can easily be taken too far and become passionate. These passionate touches should be "red flags" for the single person because they were created by God for the sole purpose of leading a married couple to experience the ultimate expression of their covenant relationship—sexual intercourse. It is hard to stop once you progress so far. It is also the nature of sexual sin (and all sin) to want to go farther the next time than you went before. Each time the boundary moves closer, it will be harder to stop.

On the board or newsprint list the possible negative and positive consequences of making decisions about crossing or not crossing the line of sexual intimacy. (Some possible consequences are listed below.) Have the students focus on the list you prepared. Say, "Every decision you make will have consequences. Decisions about how or when to use your sexuality can negatively or positively affect your body, mind, heart, and spirit. Negative consequences of crossing the line might include STDs, recurring fear of pregnancy, actual pregnancy without the support of a committed spouse, guilt, shame, and damaged relationships in the future. Positive consequences of not crossing the line include healthier relationships, true intimacy, higher self-esteem, and a richer faith."

Discuss the questions that follow with the whole group:

Why do you think God made boundaries for sexual activity? (To show us His plan for intimacy between a man and a woman; so that we might experience true love and intimacy the way He designed them to be.)

How important is it to choose a partner who shares similar values about sex? Why? (It is A LOT more difficult to resist temptation when one or both people are not committed to God's boundaries for sex.)

What activities or suggestions might help or support a couple that wants to "wait"? (Surround themselves with friends who will encourage them and hold them accountable; make definite plans for dates and limit time alone; be strengthened through regular use of the Sacraments; confess and receive absolution when temptation leads to sin; pray. Other answers may vary.)

For further information, see *The Why Files: When Can I Start Dating? Questions about Love, Sex, and a Cure for Zits* (CPH: 2000).

10 Rotten Reasons—Optional Activity (10 minutes)

Teens hear all kinds of reasons to become sexually active, without learning about any alternatives. Many of these reasons go unchallenged because of the innate sex drive that wants to be satisfied. Peer pressure can make it hard to continue to live in the grace of our Baptism without being ridiculed. It may seem that every other guy in the world but you has had sex. This is not true. This exercise will help guys openly discuss and understand what it is to live as one baptized in Christ.

The list of the "Top 10 Rotten Reasons to Have Sex" is adapted from the book *The Why Files: When Can I Start Dating? Questions about Love, Sex, and a Cure for Zits* (CPH: 2000, pp. 160–166). Each student may be provided with his own copy by reproducing Guys Student Page 3B.

Top 10 Rotten Reasons to Have Sex
To Make Love
To Prove Love
To Build Self-Esteem
To Be Socially Accepted
To "Pay" for a Date
To Prove Your Manhood
To Gain Experience
To Have a Baby
To Feel Good
To "Just Do It"

Form two groups. Have one group choose one of the "Top 10 Rotten Reasons" and use it to come up with a line that a guy may say to try to persuade a girl to have sex. Let the other group respond with an argument as to why the reason is so rotten.

Closing (2 minutes)

Reaffirm that sexual sin is a serious business that can destroy lives and faith. Strongly affirm that the forgiveness and grace of God will not restore virginity, eliminate a pregnancy, or erase emotional scars, but will sustain a relationship with the heavenly Father and give strength for a life that more closely reflects God's will.

Close this session with the following prayer: "Dear Lord, You are the maker of all good things. You have given us the gift of sexuality. We admit that we have turned this great blessing into something that sometimes brings pain. We know that You desire only the best for our lives. We thank You for Your gracious plan. By Your Spirit help us seek Your will in all that we do, that we may fully experience the goodness of Your gifts. In Jesus' name. Amen."

Paying the Price
Read 1 Corinthians 6:18–20.

Why is sex apart from marriage idolatry?

How is sexual sin different from other sins?

Why do you think this is so?

Do you agree?

What is both exciting and scary about verse 19?

How would you define temple in this context?

Why can we not do whatever we want with our body?

What was the price paid for us?

If you really believe this text, how might you respond?

Top 10 Rotten Reasons to Have Sex

To Make Love

To Prove Love

To Build Self-Esteem

To Be Socially Accepted

To "Pay" for a Date

To Prove Your Manhood

To Gain Experience

To Have a Baby

To Feel Good

To "Just Do It"

Adapted from James Watkins, *The Why Files: When Can I Start Dating? Questions about Love, Sex, and a Cure for Zits* © 2000 Concordia Publishing House.

4 FROM NOW ON

Purpose

No matter what your situation is now, things will continue to change. Our God is the Lord of life and continues to watch over us. We already live in a state of forgiveness through Holy Baptism. You may not be dating now and find this study sort of interesting but irrelevant. Some who have a handle on their sexual behavior now will continue to be tempted and may stray. Some may have already sinned sexually and may wonder if they can be forgiven or if life can be restored. All believers can have confidence that through faith in Jesus, they stand before God as perfectly forgiven by His grace through faith. In Christ we are made new. There is no difference to Him; all who confess Jesus as Lord are redeemed children of God. God can help us move beyond the past and fix our eyes on Christ and the future He has in store for us.

Gospel Emphasis

God does not condemn David, despite his adultery, but forgives him and calls him to a new commitment in His ways. This is not a license to sin, but God offers us that same gracious forgiveness for our lives.

Lesson Outline

Activity	Time Suggested	Materials Needed
Preparing for a Partner	15 minutes	note cards, markers, pens
Focus on David	25 minutes	Guys Student Page 4A
Relationship Covenant	10 minutes	Guys Student Page 4B
Six Great Reasons (optional activity)	5 minutes	Guys Student Page 4C
Closing	2 minutes	none

Preparing for a Partner (15 minutes)

It is important for guys to know what they want before they start looking for something. When seeking a wife, guys might want to identify what characteristics of a future partner are important to them. These qualities can be prayed about long before guys meet their future wife. Guys can pray that God would develop these qualities in a future partner and then lead the couple together. More importantly, guys should pray that God would shape them to be the kind of godly husband who would be a great partner in a Christian marriage. Ask the guys to write out on a note card the qualities they want in their wife. Have guys use the reverse side of the card to make a list of the characteristics they want to grow in to become the ideal Christian husband. Tell guys to be specific and refer to their lists in the future. Encourage guys to use their list while praying for their own Christian growth and that of their future partner. You may close this activity by praying as a group or in small groups for your students and their future wives.

Focus on David (25 minutes)

Ask students, "What is one thing you wanted so badly you felt you HAD to have it just to live?" (Answers will vary; maybe a toy as a kid.) "How did you handle it?" (Answers will vary. Maybe they begged and pleaded; some may even have stolen.)

Distribute copies of Guys Student Page 4A. Ask volunteers to read aloud 2 Samuel 11. Allow time for students to answer the questions from the student page, and then discuss the section as a whole group.

What was it that David felt he had to have, and how did he handle it? (Bathsheba; he took her.)

How might sex become an idol before God?

(Through the sinful desire and act of sex outside of marriage.)

How did the TLC intimacy-building elements of a relationship play out in this story?

Time—(David spent little time with her.)

Loyalty—(David was not loyal to God, to his own wives, or to his fellow soldier, Uriah. He did not encourage Bathsheba to be loyal to Uriah either.)

Communication—(We have no record of their communication until Bathsheba became pregnant.)

Touch—(It began as a purely physical relationship.)

In what ways were Uriah's actions different from David's?

(Uriah may not have done very well at spending time with Bathsheba, communicating with her, or touching her. However, this was not an excuse for her to commit adultery. Uriah did remain faithful to his men, his wife, his king, and God.)

One of the dangers of improper sexual activity is that it is sin and has the power to erode and cut off a faith relationship with God. David does not appear bothered by his sin. God becomes concerned and sends the prophet Nathan to confront David concerning his sin—a sign of God going the extra mile to restore a broken relationship with one of His beloved children. The sinner does not deserve to have God deal with him in mercy. Living in any perpetual, unconfessed sin is spiritually dangerous. We cannot simply decide to quit and be healed. It takes God's graceful action, which can be painful at times. When Nathan confronted David over his sin, David experienced the burden of guilt and sought God's forgiveness. David heard the word of God spoken through Nathan, was convicted of his sin, and received absolution. In the same way, we hear God's Word spoken by our pastor, are led to repentance, and receive Holy Absolution. David was restored and lived in God's forgiving grace. Psalm 51 was written by David as he acknowledged God's mercy.

Read together Psalm 51 and discuss the questions together.

What did God, through Nathan, lead David to do?

(Confess his sin.)

This psalm was written after David's encounter with Bathsheba. What verse best describes how you feel when you know you are guilty?

(Answers will vary. Remind students that it is not our feelings of guilt that bring about forgiveness; rather, we are forgiven because of what Christ has already done for us.)

Read aloud Psalm 32:5.

What is the outcome for David? How does this cycle also apply to us?

(God leads us to confess our sins for the purpose of receiving forgiveness. God bestows forgiveness through the blood of Jesus given in His Word and the Sacraments. It is this forgiveness that motivates new life in Christ.)

Relationship Covenant (10 minutes)

As you make a transition into the closing for this study, say, "God in His grace says that we can love because He first loved us. Christ's giving, serving, selfless love changes us to be like Him. It also guides our actions and decisions, as He gives us patience to wait for His blessing, and strength to resist temptation in the meantime. Our lives are a reflection of what Christ has worked in us in our Baptism. Our sexuality is as powerful as it is unique. The power of the Holy Spirit helps us to guard against going outside of God's desire for how we use this gift. Through a faith relationship with God, as His Spirit continues to work in our lives, sin no longer has control over us."

This activity is designed to remind students that it is only with the power of God that we can overcome temptation in our lives; without Him we are helpless. Distribute copies of Guys Student Page 4B. Say, "This covenant is a reminder of the covenant that God established with us in our Baptism to make us His sons. Throughout the Bible and in Holy Communion, He reminds us of this relationship that He established with us and empowers us to have healthier relationships with those around us." Encourage students to pray silently for God to guide their use of His gift of sexuality, and then complete and sign the covenant form.

Six Great Reasons—Optional Activity (5 minutes)

The list of "Six Great Reasons to Have Sex" is adapted from and explained in greater detail in the book *The Why Files: When Can I Start Dating? Questions about Love, Sex, and a Cure for Zits* (CPH: 2000, pp. 166–71). By reproducing Guys Student Page 4C, each student may receive his own copy. Use the list as a discussion starter with the students. Invite them to post this reminder at home. Ask how each of the statements can affect their lives.

Six Great Reasons to Have Sex
To Express Love for Your Bride as Christ Has for His Bride, the Church
To Express a Lifelong Commitment
To Express a Lifelong Love
To Give and Receive Pleasure
To Grow Closer Together Mentally, Emotionally, and Spiritually
To Bring New Life into the World

Use this as a discussion starter with the students. How can each of the statements affect their lives?

Closing (2 minutes)

Close this session with the following prayer: "Most loving Father, Your grace is beyond our imagination. You have shown Your love to all people through the work of Your Son. Please forgive us for the times we have strayed outside of Your will for our lives. We admit that our way is wrong and Your way is right. Thank You for desiring to offer grace and every blessing to each and every one of us, and for giving us Your Word to reveal Yourself and draw us closer to You. Thank You for the forgiveness You freely offer to us. We ask that You would be truly present in and strengthen our relationships. Remind us daily of Your incredible relationship with us. Through Jesus Christ we pray. Amen."

Focus on David
Read 2 Samuel 11.

What was it that David felt he had to have, and how did he handle it?

How might sex become an idol before God?

How did the TLC intimacy-building elements of a relationship play out in this story?

    Time?

    Loyalty?

    Communication?

    Touch?

In what ways were Uriah's actions different from David's?

Look at Psalm 51.

What did God, through Nathan, lead David to do?

This psalm was written after David's encounter with Bathsheba. What verse best describes you when you know you are guilty?

What was the outcome for David? How does this cycle also apply to us?

I, _____, realize that my body is

not my own. I was bought with a price. At my Baptism God placed

His name upon my heart and made me His child. He wants what is

best for me and desires that all my actions, words, and even my

thoughts be pleasing in His sight. He is the perfect, loving Father and He

forgives me, no matter what I have done. I know that what is past is for-

given through God's graceful act of faith in Christ, and God has given me a

clean slate, a new beginning each day. With this covenant I remember the

relationship that God has established with me, and I ask God to help me

never to replace that bond with any girl here on earth. I acknowledge that it

is most important that God's relationship with me come before all others.

With God's help I will honor the body He has given me for His glory.

Signed _____ Date_____

Six Great Reasons to Have Sex

**To Express Love for Your Bride
as Christ Has for His Bride, the Church**

To Express a Lifelong Commitment

To Express a Lifelong Love

To Give and Receive Pleasure

**To Grow Closer Together
Mentally, Emotionally, and Spiritually**

To Bring New Life into the World

Excerpted from James Watkins, *The Why Files: When Can I Start
Dating? Questions about Love, Sex, and a Cure for Zits*
© 2000 Concordia Publishing House.

Additional Resources

Additional materials for use with *Guy Stuff: Dating and Sexuality* are available from Concordia Publishing House at no additional charge. Simply visit the CPH Web site at www.cph.org/youth/guygirl/dating.

Girl Stuff:

Dating and Sexuality

CPH®

Concordia Publishing House

Author: Beth Murphy

Editor: Mark Sengele

Your comments and suggestions concerning this material are appreciated. Please write the Editor of Youth Materials, Concordia Publishing House, 3558 S. Jefferson Avenue, St. Louis, MO 63118-3968.

This publication is also available in braille and in large type for the visually impaired. Call 1-800-433-3954 or write to Library for the Blind, 1333 S. Kirkwood Rd., St. Louis, MO 63122-7295.

Scripture taken from the HOLY BIBLE, NEW INTERNATIONAL VERSION®. NIV®.
Copyright © 1973, 1978, 1984 by International Bible Society.
Used by permission of Zondervan Publishing House. All rights reserved.

Copyright © 2002 Concordia Publishing House
3558 S. Jefferson Avenue, St. Louis, MO 63118-3968
Manufactured in the United States of America

1 2 3 4 5 6 7 8 9 10   11 10 09 08 07 06 05 04 03 02

Contents

The Perfect Date 1

Purpose

Every young woman wants to be known and loved deeply by a significant person. While family members play an important role in an adolescent's life, a young woman will eventually look beyond the family for someone else. There may be many reasons why you want to date. God created male and female with a desire for each other that is still present, even though it has been drastically altered after the fall into sin. Love relationships often begin by dating. But before we can analyze dating, we must ask, what *is* dating anyway? Is it a rite of passage? Is it just a pastime? Is it an innate drive? Confusion about the purpose of dating may lead some girls to foster unrealistic expectations that may complicate future relationships. Because the first dating experience sets the pattern for what follows, girls should know from the start what God's will is for their dating life. Often there is no Dating 101 class for them to learn what to do and how to act. This study addresses some of the issues from that kind of class.

Gospel Emphasis

God in His love desires to have a relationship with each one of us and for that reason sent Jesus to make that relationship possible. Christ died for all of us, regardless of how we look or how funny we act sometimes.

Lesson Outline

Activity	Time Suggested	Materials Needed
Dating Game	15 minutes	newsprint with topic list
Speak Your Mind (optional activity)	10 minutes	bag of topics
What about Me?	15 minutes	Girls Student Page 1A
Pyramid Production (optional activity)	15 minutes	see intructions
Song of Songs	20 minutes	Girls Student Page 1B
The Perfect Date	10 minutes	newsprint, markers
Closing	2 minutes	none

Dating Game (15 minutes)

This activity is designed to get girls thinking about how to identify an appropriate date. This will be very effective if you have a group that likes to share stories. List on newsprint or a board the topics listed below:

Meeting his parents
Deciding what to do
Determining who pays
Dealing with curfews
Saying goodbyes
Deciding where to go
Daring to give the first kiss

Use these topics to discuss what goes into a date or to describe the perfect date. Ask students to discuss dates they have been on or heard about. (Caution students to avoid gossip.) What went well? What didn't work? What can they learn from these past experiences? What is their ideal in each of these areas? Try to draw some conclusions about what makes good or bad dates. Example: Good dates give you the opportunity to talk and get to know each other. Bad dates are where you can't talk (for instance, at movies or dances). There is more to a date than "hooking up."

Speak Your Mind—Optional Activity (10 minutes)

Fill a paper bag with paper slips or note cards with topics from the "Dating Game" activity. You may add your own topics if you like. Invite one student at a time to come up and select a topic from the bag. Students must then give a 60-second impromptu speech about their topic. Speeches may include do's and don'ts, other advice, or past history. After the speeches, discuss any new insights and get reactions.

What about Me? (15 minutes)

Ever been to a potluck? Lots of people bring lots of different foods, and everybody goes back for lots of seconds of the things they liked. Let's face it: dating other people can be a little like a potluck. Different people increase our exposure to different things. Being open to new things is a fun part of dating. Who knows? After trying a new activity, hobby, music, or food, you may decide that you think it's great or you "kinda" like it or you can barely stand it or you HATE it!

But some things are part of who we are and should not be compromised—things like VALUES and GOALS. Through our Baptism we gain a baptismal identity. God makes us His very children and as a result we share values that are different from the world's values. As Christians our values and goals are shaped by our Christian faith.

This activity is designed to encourage girls to more deeply develop an idea of who they are and what they value. This very important process serves as a foundation for decisions they will make in current or future relationships. Identifying core values, goals, and beliefs will help a young woman to see herself as God does—as His baptized, redeemed child. Recognizing this fact allows young women to seek a partner who shares

The topic of date rape may come up in the process of sharing. It is suggested that you research this and other topics beforehand to support you in giving answers to tough questions. Resources to facilitate discussion concerning rape and other critical issues include *The Why Files: When Can I Start Dating? Questions about Love, Sex, and a Cure for Zits* (CPH: 2000) and *Love, Sex, and God* (CPH: 1998).

common values, to set boundaries for sexual activity, and to more easily reject cheap substitutes for real love. Girls' expectations of who they should be is too often influenced by pop culture, trying to measure up to peer-group expectations, or the notion of the "ideal" woman found in magazines. This activity will help girls to see what God has made them to be in Holy Baptism. Remind them that their goals and values can reflect God's will for all believers (Matthew 10:29–31).

Hand out copies of Girls Student Page 1A. Say, "A once-popular country song states, 'You've got to stand for something, or you'll fall for anything.' Why do you think it might be important to clarify your values before you start dating?" Guide the responses toward the conclusions listed above. Have the girls break into small groups to answer the questions on the student page and then share within their group. After breakout groups have shared, ask for some responses to be shared with the larger group.

Once the students have finished the five-year goals, say, "All that we have is a gift from God! And He has blessed you with so much, including a great potential future! We are to take care of all His gifts to us, including our sexuality. It is one of the most powerful gifts given to us by God. With this in mind, how can you best use the gift of sexuality over the next five years? How about over a lifetime?"

This activity is designed to help your students better understand the factors that influence the choices they make. You may want to incorporate a personality inventory into this activity just to help them begin to think about how each person has different strengths, interests, and abilities.

Pyramid Production—Optional Activity (15 minutes)

Preparation: Assemble "building" materials beforehand such as canned goods, empty (but clean) food containers, small toys, fruit, and so on. Your goal is to select items in different forms, weights, and sizes. Use your imagination and creatively arrange the junk-on-hand.

Divide the class into groups of two to four people. Give groups five minutes to construct a pyramid that has five or more levels. The goal is to create a structure that is as tall and strong as possible using at least five different building materials. After five minutes have passed, let each group evaluate their structure on both strength and height using a 1–10 scale (1=weakest, smallest; 10=sturdiest, tallest). Follow up by discussing these questions: Which building material was most important for your pyramid to achieve it's maximum height and strength? How might this task have been different without a solid base? What purpose does a good foundation have? (Provides stability for everything built upon it.)

After allowing for discussion, read the parable of the wise and foolish builders found in Luke 6:47–49. Say, "A solid foundation is necessary for any building project. The foundation of a strong, secure relationship with others begins with a strong relationship with God in Christ. We love because He first loved us. The most healthy relationships also rise above our own sins and needs, rooted in God's forgiveness and built upon who God made you to be. God started laying that foundation in Baptism, which shapes goals and values. A combination of time, loyalty, and communication builds intimacy and security in relationships with God and others."

Song of Songs (20 minutes)

Distribute copies of Girls Student Page 1B to each student. This study highlights God's intimate relationship with us and encourages girls to prepare for a future exclusive relationship by practicing the same concepts in their social relationships.

Dating takes time and does not produce an instant relationship. As teens begin dating, they are influenced by how others perceive them. Teens need to be reminded the truth that who they are in Christ greatly impacts or determines what they do. Personal identity is a powerful factor is in dating. How much more so is the new identity our Lord gives us when He adopts us as His very own family and declares us righteous.

The intimacy and security in a strong relationship need some TLC in order to grow: time, loyalty, and communication. As sinners we are unable to manage on our own. It is only in Christ that all relationships are restored and make perfect. God's plan for this kind of intimacy in a marriage relationship is shown in the example of the beloved and the lover in the Song of Songs (Song of Solomon). Developing and managing TLC in an exclusive relationship can be a lot of work. As sinners, we are unable to manage on our own. It is only in Christ that all relationships are restored and made perfect. Teens can learn aspects of it as they practice applying these concepts in their social relationships and early, less-committed dating relationships.

Have the students study each of the Bible passages listed on the student page. Each verse gives an example of time, loyalty, or communication. Encourage the group to relate the verses to the given topic. Have them record their answers on the student page and share them with the group. Once students have shared their answers, read or summarize the explanation for each section below.

Some Thoughts Concerning Relationships

Time

Song of Songs 2:10–13; 7:11–12. It would be hard to say that you have a close relationship with a person you never spend time with. A relationship is built over time by exploring common interests, getting to know a person's likes and dislikes, and observing how that person acts in social situations.

Do you think the saying "Quality, not quantity" is true concerning time spent in relationships? Why or why not? (Both quality and quantity of time are needed for a growing relationship.) In fact, it may take lots of time (a great quantity) to achieve some good quality time.

Loyalty

Song of Songs 1:5–6. Loyalty means acting with truthfulness and not betraying another's trust. Often dating relationships contain partial truths, outright lies, exaggerated stories, or false claims because people are afraid to reveal who they really are. The beloved here does not try to puff herself up to be something she is not. She admits her shortcomings and does not paint a false picture. In spite of the risk, she is still adored by friends and her lover. Each individual is known completely by God. God intentionally made each of us different for His purpose, and we must not be afraid to let

someone know how unique we really are. A strong relationship built on loyalty begins with honesty, integrity, and trustworthiness.

What potential problems in a relationship might be avoided by acting in truth and honesty with respect to who God made you to be? (Answers will vary.)

Communication

Song of Songs 1:15–16. The Book of Song of Songs is a dialogue between the beloved and the lover (with side comments from friends), which illustrates the importance of conversation in building a relationship. Conversation that builds intimacy should probe beneath a person's obvious likes and dislikes to explore their personal goals, spiritual maturity, and values.

Getting some guys to open up about personal things like values and beliefs can be a challenge. No one may feel comfortable at first, until some initial foundation stones can be laid. What can you do to make it easier? (Possible answers: be an active listener, be willing to share first, be patient.)

Some Thoughts Concerning God's Relationship with Us

Now look at each of the corresponding verses and themes as they relate to our faith life. God wants relationships between His people to reflect His relationship with us through Jesus Christ, His Son. The Bible says Jesus is the groom and the church is His bride. What an amazing example Jesus gives us of what it means to be loved deeply and completely. The following verses will show how God has displayed TLC to us. How is the theme demonstrated in each verse?

Time

Psalm 16:11; 84:10. God is not bound by time like we are. His desire isn't that we just spend some quality time with Him, but He desires for us to be in His presence for all eternity. Jesus' mission on earth made that a reality for us. In the meantime, the best way to experience His intimate love occurs when the Holy Spirit works in you as you spend time in His Word, in prayer, in worship, in Communion, and by living out His grace that first came in your Baptism.

How has God given quality time or quantity of time in developing a relationship with us, His people? (Both quality and quantity come through worship, Scripture, and other significant life/faith experiences.)

Loyalty

Psalm 32:5. The closeness of a relationship can be directly correlated to the level of loyalty and truth between people in that relationship. God works in our lives, helping us to be open and honest with Him (He already knows everything about us) in a way that clears away the garbage of sin between us. Remember the beloved's rating of her own beauty? We, too, see our ugliness of sin. The great news is that God puts us in a new standing before Him by the work of Jesus Christ and says, "I love you and want to be with you," and we can now see our standing before Him in a new light. God sees the beauty of Christ reflected in us. And this Gospel truth must be lived out in our lives—for example, in how we treat others in a dating relationship.

What does God's loyalty mean to you? (Answers will vary.)

Communication

Jeremiah 29:11–13; 1 Thessalonians 5:17. God has in mind the perfect plan for your life, including your dating life. Do you want to know what it is? We know that His plan is for you to have a relationship with Him in this life and throughout eternity. Other details unfold over time as He guides our lives through faith. Talk to Him. Tell Him what's on your mind. Share your "what ifs?" and your "what nows?" His unchanging, eternal promise is that He will be found by you and will hear your prayers. He guides your faith and works through His Word to direct your decisions, lifestyle choices, and directions.

In what other ways does God communicate with us? (Scripture shows a past, present, and future glimpse of God's great love for you. In Baptism God says, "You are My child." Through Holy Communion God says, "You are My honored guest. I forgive you and will strengthen you.")

The Perfect Date (10 minutes)

Often expectations are set so high for dates that everything seems to fall short. This activity will help girls evaluate what is important in a date and how to accomplish it. You will need newsprint and markers. Use this as a brainstorming session. On one side write "Goals" and on the other side write "Plans."

First discuss the purpose of dating and put these thoughts under "Goals." Tell the students to look at what they want to accomplish. Is the purpose of a date to get to know another person, to have fun, to avoid loneliness, to feel loved, or . . . what? Because certain goals, like sexual activity, can be outside of God's boundaries, share that goals should demonstrate a respect for God, others, and self. Once you have some goals written down, start asking for ways to accomplish those goals and list them under "Plans." You should begin to develop a pretty good selection of dating ideas. Tell the group that the perfect date would be one where God's work is evident and His name is praised through us and our behavior.

Closing (2 minutes)

Close this session with the following prayer: "Heavenly Father, Your love for us cannot be matched. Forgive us for not loving You or others like You loved us. We thank You for accepting us as we are and desiring and empowering the best in all we do. May Your Spirit live in our lives that we may continue to develop the connection You have made with us. Through Your Son, Jesus Christ, we pray. Amen."

What about Me?

How would you describe yourself to an Internet chat-room friend?

What is your favorite characteristic about yourself?

List your strengths, interests, and abilities. What don't you like to do?

In each of the categories listed below, list two goals you want to accomplish in the next five years.

Personal Life:

 Academic

 Career

 Relationships

Spiritual life:

 Prayer

 Bible Study

 Worship

 Lifestyle

For what areas of your sexuality do you most thank God? For what do you want His help in the area of your sexuality over the next five years? During your lifetime? How might your attitudes and actions expressing your sexuality during the next five years affect the rest of your life?

Some Thoughts Concerning Relationships

Time, loyalty, and communication are needed in developing and maintaining a good relationship. We can see from the Song of Songs that all of these elements are present.

Look at each of the corresponding themes and verses. How is the theme demonstrated in each verse?

Time
Song of Songs 2:10–13; 7:11–12
Do you think the saying "Quality, not quantity" is true concerning time spent in relationships? Why or why not?

Loyalty
Song of Songs 1:5–6
What potential problems in a relationship might be avoided by acting in truth and honesty with respect to who God made you to be?

Communication
Song of Songs 1:15–16
Getting some guys to open up about personal things like values and beliefs can be a challenge. What can you do to make it easier?

Now look back over your answers and each theme. How do you feel about these characteristics, and do you think they are important? Why?

Some Thoughts Concerning God's Relationship with Us

Now look at each of the corresponding verses and themes as they relate to our faith life. God wants relationships between people to be modeled after His relationship with us through Jesus Christ, His Son. The Bible says that Christ is the groom and the church is His bride. What an amazing example Jesus gives us of what it means to be loved deeply and completely.

The following verses will show how God has displayed TLC to us. How is the theme demonstrated in each verse?

Time
Psalm 16:11; 84:10
How has God given quality time or quantity of time in developing a relationship with us, His people?

Loyalty
Psalm 32:5
What does God's loyalty mean to you?

Communication
Jeremiah 29:11–13; 1 Thessalonians 5:17
In what other ways does God communicate with us?

Looking back at these answers, we see that God has been gracious throughout human history, extending also to us. In response to His love and filled with His Spirit, we can show TLC to those around us. How can you demonstrate TLC in the relationships in your life?

A Perfect Love 2

Purpose

Many young women looking for love are looking to connect with someone. They want the intimacy that comes from being deeply loved and accepted, but may not know the means to that end. Peers and the media may offer misleading and conflicting guidance, complicating the matter even further. Girls may ask: How do I know if I can trust this person? How do I know when love is real? How do we stay in love? There is a shortage of healthy relationships in the world for them to learn from. Even biblical characters provide a picture of fallen man in a struggle to relate. Only God demonstrates a perfect example of divine love and the nature of a healthy relationship with others.

Gospel Emphasis

We have the perfect heavenly Father, who loves unconditionally. Living in His love in Christ, we are enabled to feel good about who we are as God's creatures, forgiven and given unique gifts, talents, and abilities. God's love makes it possible for us to make God-pleasing decisions concerning our relationships. The more we respect ourselves and others as God's children, the more respectfully we will relate to others.

Lesson Outline

Activity	Time Suggested	Materials Needed
Either/Or (optional activity)	10 minutes	marker board or newsprint
What's in a Friend?	15 minutes	newsprint, markers
Love Is—Part 1	15 minutes	Girls Student Page 2A
Examples of Love	10 minutes	none
Love Is—Part 2	20 minutes	Girls Student Page 2B
Closing	2 minutes	none

Either/Or—Optional Activity (10 minutes)

This activity is designed to get girls thinking and talking about the qualities they look for when making a friend. It is also intended to help girls to discover that many of the same characteristics found in a good female friend are also important for a good relationship with a guy. Most girls talk openly about friends and friendship. Try to create a "safe" place for students to share their thoughts. This may be done by modeling such behavior yourself. You may want to describe a close friend you have and why this person is your friend.

List on newsprint or a marker board the qualities given below. You may want to reveal only one choice at a time. Have students move to one side of the room or the other depending upon their response to the question "Which of these two characteristics is most important as you look for a friend?" Ask students to give reasons for their choice. Once you have completed all four choice pairs, ask the question "What qualities do you think God looks for in people?"

- creativity or humor?
- looks or personality?
- popularity or generosity?
- hygiene or thoughtfulness?

What's in a Friend? (15 minutes)

When a girl says, "Let's just be friends," to a guy she is usually ringing a "death knell" to what might have been a possible relationship. Let's face it. For guys, friendship with a girl is not the first thing that comes to mind. However, a meaningful friendship within a relationship is what most young women really want. Young women want to have a relationship with someone who will also be their best friend. This activity is designed to remind young women that it is not unrealistic to have relationships with guys who are also their friends.

Divide students into small groups. Provide each group a sheet of newsprint and markers. Say, "Your assignment is to come up with two lists of characteristics. One list should describe your best friend. The other should describe your ideal boyfriend. Try to rank the characteristics in order of importance." Give girls seven or eight minutes to develop their lists. Invite the groups back together to share their lists. Ask, "Where do the qualities you listed differ between a friend and a boyfriend? Where are they similar? Why do you think it might be important to have a boyfriend who is a friend as well?"

Love Is—Part 1 (15 minutes)

Distribute copies of Girls Student Page 2A. Read together 1 Corinthians 13:1–8a. Allow students time to answer the questions from the student page. Guide a discussion of their findings following these suggestions:

Whom is the apostle Paul speaking of in this passage?
(Christ)
How has this been expressed?
(In Christ's keeping the Law on our behalf and His selfless sacrifice upon the cross for our sake.)
How do you receive this love in order to reflect it to others?
(This love is given solely by God's grace and forgiveness given in our Baptism.)
How might people express their love for someone? (Answers will vary. The text suggests through words, personal characteristics, and the giving of gifts.)
What have you done to show someone that you love them? (Answers will vary.)

What would you say is the main point of verses 1 to 3? (We have a variety of gifts and talents, but they don't mean much if we don't use them sincerely in love for others. In this way love is one of the most important things we can possess.)

List the seven things that describe what love is and the nine things that love is not. (Love is patient, kind, joyful in truth, protecting, trusting, hopeful, and persevering. Love is not envious, boastful, proud, rude, self-seeking, easily angered, interested in keeping a record of wrongs, delighting in evil, and capable of failing.)

How do these compare with relationships that you have been in and others you've seen? (Answers will vary. Go down the list if the group is having difficulties.)

Examples of Love (10 minutes)

Ask each student to think of a person who demonstrates the best example of love. Make sure that each student has a definite person in mind before you divide the students into pairs and have each student tell her partner about the loving person she chose to describe. After five minutes or so, go around the room and have each person share as much about her loving example as she feels comfortable sharing.

Say, "We all have loving people who touch our lives, but not as many as we should. Many people love with selfish attitudes and actions. Sinful people can never give perfect love. There is only One who has ever done that, Jesus Christ. God gives us the picture of perfect love in His Word. His perfect love is *agape*, a completely selfless and giving love that only seeks good for the receiver. In studying 1 Corinthians 13, we see that Jesus fulfills the description of love perfectly."

Love Is—Part 2 (20 minutes)

Hand out copies of Girls Student Page 2B to each student. Allow students time to work together in small groups to study how Christ fulfilled each characteristic of love listed in 1 Corinthians 13. After allowing time for groups to study, use these notes to lead a discussion with the whole group. Remember to point out at each example that Jesus is much more than a role model who fulfills the Law for us. He is perfect love, and He lived in perfect love for us. He forgives our failure to live up to these characteristics. He also helps us to grow and better live in His perfect love with others.

Love Is Patient

Instant gratification is a part of our culture. From modems to McDonald's, things just aren't fast enough to satisfy us. Guys (and girls too!) sometimes want to dive straight into sexual intimacy. Girls may also expect relational intimacy (trust and security) from the beginning of a relationship. Being patient often means setting our own needs aside to wait for a greater good. Jesus understood this: in Matthew 4:1–4, Jesus could have instantly satisfied His hunger pangs by giving in to Satan's temptation. The salvation of the entire world depended on His living a life without sin. For God's greater good, Jesus waited for His needs to be filled in the Father's time.

How might patience lead to a greater good in a love relationship? (God promises to bless those who wait on His timing and plans for a relationship.)

Love Is Kind

Have you experienced any unexplainable "random acts of kindness"? Whether you have been the giver or the receiver, you might have experienced some benefit. In a recent popular movie the main character does a favor for three different people without expecting a favor in return. These people are moved by this act of kindness, and instead of paying the favor back, they "pay it forward" to three others in need—beginning a chain reaction.

True love is not only a feeling; it's also an action. God's kind of love is sensitive to the needs of girls and guys. He acts through the kind of love that Jesus shows us in Matthew 14:14.

Why are acts of kindness so powerful? How might kindness transform a relationship? (An act of kindness can soften a hardened heart. It provides an opportunity for the believer to share the Gospel with those who are being served.)

Love Is Humble

There are only two adjectives that Jesus uses to describe Himself in the New Testament. They both occur in Matthew 11:29. Imagine a king who trades his crown for street clothes and who goes to the impoverished parts of town to provide all-you-can-eat buffets for the people. Imagine that he sits down in the street to eat and talk with them. He is highly educated, but speaks simply so the common people will understand about his justice and mercy, his laws and his love. He knows his own worth, his value, and yet he gives every single person his attention as if he were speaking to his most highly honored guest. There is no envy, boastfulness, or pride. There is only love. The disciple John speaks of Jesus in this way in John 13:3–5, 12–17.

Why is humility so hard for most of us to express? What does the world think of humbleness? (Because of our sinful nature, humility is difficult for many people. The world perceives humility as a sign of weakness. God's Word shows us Christ's strength in His humility.)

Love Is Selfless

Often our sinful nature causes us to enter into a relationship to see what we can get out of it. Some may do so just to be sexually gratified. Others may think that a relationship could raise their social acceptability or boost self-esteem. We all tend to be high on the taking and low on the giving side of things. The saying "What have you done for me lately?" is an indication of this tendency. Thankfully God has given up His all for us. He set the example of a selfless and giving love. We can only give to Him out of what He has given to us. Jesus gave up everything, even His life, for our salvation. In Romans 5:7–8 we are reminded that Christ died for us, in spite of who we are, while we are still sinners. He received nothing in return for His act of selflessness. We can demonstrate that love to those around us as the Holy Spirit strengthens us for service.

What do you think a relationship would be like if both people involved were completely selfless? (While our sinful nature makes this impossible, relationships that include selfless love for each other are often very strong.)

Love Is Forgiving and Encouraging

Relationships are ruined by offenses that are never forgotten. Families may have members that have not spoken for years because of an argument that was never resolved. Put-downs and pointed fingers can also keep intimacy from growing. When forgiveness and encouragement abound, there can be healthy growth in relationships, even in tough times. It is best when we can continue to have a friendly relationship with a guy whom we once dated. When we treat others respectfully, we have a better chance of relationships ending peacefully, even when there is pain. God in His mercy has not held back His forgiveness and encouragement from us, although we are entirely at fault. In John 8:2–11, Jesus would have had the authority to condemn the woman caught in adultery for her offense, and yet He forgave her. We sin greatly; we are also greatly forgiven and encouraged to live in the light of His love. By God's grace we won't take His forgiveness for granted and lose our desire to try to live for Him. 1 Thessalonians 3:11–13 reminds us of how much God desires to bless us.

How does this truth encourage us each day? (We know that Jesus forgives each time we need it. By His grace, He continues to shower us with His love.)

Love Is Forever

Can anything last forever? Our culture is marked by short-lived and disposable things: pre-made meals, single-use disposable cameras, seasonal fashions, and changing fads. This trend is also seen in relationships, as many marriages end in divorce. If love is conditional, once the affection and feelings wear off, there is little need for the partner anymore. Thanks be to God that His love for us is without condition, bound by His unbreakable promise or covenant. Jesus' last words to His bride, the church, tenderly reflect this perfect love in Matthew 28:20.

How does it feel to know that God will always love you perfectly and completely? How might this strengthen you in a relationship? How might it encourage you when you are not in a relationship? (Knowing that we are perfectly loved empowers us to share this love with others. It also reminds us that even if we aren't in a relationship with another person, we are still greatly loved.)

Closing (2 minutes)

Close this session with the following prayer: "Heavenly Father, You have developed a perfect relationship with us in Jesus Christ. We confess that we often look other places to find relationships before we look to You. Lord, thank You for calling us by name and making us Yours in Baptism. Remind us daily of this relationship, and guide us in our interactions with those around us. In Jesus' name we pray. Amen."

Love Is—Part 1
Read 1 Corinthians 13:1–8a.

Whom is the apostle Paul speaking of in this passage?

How has this been expressed?

How do we receive this love in order to reflect it to others?

How do people express their love for someone?

What have you done to show someone that you love them?

What would you say is the main point of verses 1 to 3?

List the seven things that describe what love is and the nine things that love is not.

How do these compare with your relationships and those you have seen involving others?

Love Is—Part 2

We have a God who is Love. He is the perfect fulfillment of 1 Corinthians 13. Look at these examples of how Jesus showed perfect love throughout His earthly ministry. Read the selected verses and describe how Jesus fulfilled each characteristic of love.

Love Is Patient • Matthew 4:1–11
How might patience lead to a greater good in a love relationship?

_____

Love Is Kind • Matthew 14:14
Why are acts of kindness so powerful? How might kindness transform a relationship?

_____

Love Is Humble • Matthew 11:29; John 13:3–5, 12–17
Why is humility so hard for most of us to express? What does the world think of humbleness?

_____

Love Is Selfless • Romans 5:7–8; John 15:13
What do you think a relationship would be like if both people involved were completely selfless?

_____

Love Is Forgiving and Encouraging • John 8:2–11; 1 Thessalonians 3:11–13
How does this truth encourage us each day?

_____

Love Is Forever • Matthew 28:20
How does it feel to know that God will always love you perfectly and completely? How might this strengthen you in a relationship? How might it encourage you when you are not in a relationship?

_____

3 Just Do It?

Purpose

In a "just do it" culture that targets teens, girls are bombarded with images and messages that misrepresent love as sex. Because of the nonchalant attitude our society holds toward premarital sex, girls who do not claim to be sexually active are open to ridicule and misunderstanding. In reality, there is much more to lose than to gain by becoming sexually active. The reality is that young women will not gain lasting or fulfilling respect or importance by becoming sexually active. Premarital sex usually lowers self-respect, increases fear and insecurity, and reduces a girl's feeling of value and importance. Sex was designed by God as an expression of covenant love, a love that mirrors His love for us.

Gospel Emphasis

God wants only the best for us as His children. He loves us so much that He tells us what is going to be best for us as sexual beings. He promises never to allow us to be tempted beyond what we can bear, and He forgives us when we are weak.

Lesson Outline

Activity	Time Suggested	Materials Needed
TLC Toss	15 minutes	tennis ball, alarm clock, phone receiver, journal, precious object
Paying the Price	15 minutes	Girls Student Page 3A
Making a Level Table	15 minutes	newsprint/board, small table (optional)
How Far Can I Go?	15 minutes	newsprint/board
10 Rotten Reasons (optional activity)	10 minutes	Girls Student Page 3B
Closing	2 minutes	none

TLC Toss (15 minutes)

This activity is designed to reinforce the idea that relationships take TLC (time, loyalty, and communication). It will demonstrate that trying to "juggle" all of the elements of a relationship can be harder than it seems. Relationships take work and practice. They get even tougher when you add physical touch and contact to the equation. You will need the four items listed below. A deeper explanation of each item also follows.

Form groups of six to eight people and have them sit or stand in a circle, allowing for some elbow room. Tell the groups they will be tossing an object to other group members across from them following these guide-

lines: Objects may not be tossed to a person more than once until everyone has had a turn. Students will always toss the object to the same person. The leader should help establish the pattern. You may want to practice with a tennis ball until groups get the hang of the pattern. The game becomes more difficult as additional objects (from the list below) are added and used simultaneously.

Order	Suggested Object	Represents
first	alarm clock	time
second	journal	loyalty
third	phone receiver	communication
fourth	precious object*	touch

* Choose something fragile with sentimental attachment, such as an heirloom. Don't worry! This object will not actually be thrown into the rotation, but will serve as a catalyst for the discussion.

As each item is tossed into the rotation, review these intimacy-building concepts:

Time (alarm clock)

A relationship begins by spending meaningful time with someone. This does not include time spent touching or kissing. An activity that allows you to explore common interests, to get to know a guy's likes and dislikes, or to see how he acts in social situations is time well spent.

Loyalty (journal)

Loyalty means to remain committed to something or someone. It involves keeping someone's trust. In a relationship you need to be open and share personal thoughts, opinions, and feelings—gently and truthfully, as you would do in a journal. Too often girls in a relationship feel the need to put up a false front in order to be accepted. In reality, by trying to fit in, we may blend in so well we aren't noticed or appreciated as individuals. We need not be afraid to let others know how unique, amazing, and even complex God has made us. Each person is an individual who is completely known and loved by God. The foundation for a strong relationship is built with loyalty. The journal symbolizes loyalty and trust between people.

Communication (phone receiver)

Talking and listening play an important part in getting to know someone. Conversation that builds intimacy probes beneath the obvious likes and dislikes of a person and explores more of their personal goals, reveals their level of spiritual maturity, and presents their value system. It takes time to achieve this, especially since some guys may hesitate to open up in this way. Be patient!

Touch (precious object)

We've learned that a relationship takes TLC. But once a relationship progresses, it starts to involve a fourth element, touch. Some touching may seem like no big deal to girls, but it can be a different story for guys who are wired to be more turned on by it. Along with time, loyalty, and communication, touch is an important part in a relationship. Touch also potentially has great consequences.

Touch is an important part of a relationship, but if it is misused, it can also diminish or destroy a couple's intimacy. Like this valuable heirloom, God made our sexuality unique and precious. Because it involves and impacts one's entire body, soul, heart, and mind, it needs to be handled so carefully that it is not damaged. God's intention is that full, intimate

touch be handled with awe and respect only within the realm of total commitment—marriage. Because some girls may attempt to find their self-worth through their relationships with guys, they may more easily accept sex as a cheap substitute for real love. Remind your students that they are extremely valuable and loved by God Himself; therefore, they should act and expect to be treated with the same regard.

Paying the Price (15 minutes)

For Further Discussion
In what ways might sexuality be handled carelessly by a guy or girl? (Sexual involvement begins too quickly and progresses too far, not requiring a trust-and-commitment level, taking a risk that sounds fun. Answers may vary.)
What might be another definition of total commitment outside marriage? (None. Saying, "But we love each other," getting engaged, or living together to determine compatibility are typically used to rationalize sexual intimacy. All these reasons fall short of the commitment in a covenant relationship that God intended us to experience; sexual relations outside of marriage is idolatry.)

Distribute copies of Girls Student Page 3A. Encourage students to read and study 1 Corinthians 6:18–20 and respond to the questions in small groups. After allowing time for groups to work, discuss the findings with the whole group.

Why is sex apart from marriage idolatry?

(Sexual activity outside of the boundaries of marriage is sin. Sin displaces God in our lives and is idolatry.)

How is sexual sin different from other sins? (Sexual sin is against the body, which is a temple of God that is miraculously able to become one with another person through sexual intercourse. Becoming one is not to be taken lightly—a breakup can leave both lives emotionally shattered.)

Why do you think this is so? (Answers will vary; see the answer above.)

Do you agree? (Answers will vary.)

What is both exciting and scary about verse 19? (The fact that God dwells inside of us can convict us, but also can provide a source of great strength and encouragement.)

How would you define *temple* in this context? (Answers will vary. A place where God chooses to dwell.)

Why can we not do what we want with our body? (It is not ours; we were bought with a price.)

What was the price paid for us? (Jesus' life given on the cross—see 1 Peter 1:18–19.)

If you really believe this text, how could you respond? (With guilty conviction because of our sin, but in joyful freedom in the forgiveness of God.)

Making a Level Table (15 minutes)

On newsprint or a marker board draw a picture of a table, showing all four legs. On each leg write one of the following: *commitment, communication, time,* and *physical contact.* Talk about how a level table is balanced, with each leg of the table being as long as the others. A healthy relationship should be similarly balanced. Physical contact can be extended fully only when commitment is also extended fully. God has established that full commitment exists only in marriage, and full physical expression through sexual intercourse should wait until then. When any component of a relationship is extended farther than the level of commitment, there are negative effects emotionally, physically, and spiritually. God wired us that way. Explore some possible problems that might occur if a relationship doesn't have the proper balance. Talk about how to prevent these

problems. Encourage girls to see that they can hardly have a full commitment to a relationship during their high school years, which means that other aspects of the relationship need to be held back as well. Even engagement is not a full commitment; engagements are often broken.

How Far Can I Go? (15 minutes)

Ironically, this question is sometimes asked after teens have already stepped over the line they had established in their conscience. Our conscience is a God-given gift that can guide us to make and stick with God-pleasing decisions. However, even our conscience feels the effects of sin. Sometimes our mind works hard to rationalize sin and ignore the alarm bells of a guilty conscience. When we rationalize sin, it chips away at our conscience's ability to steer us to make wise decisions. Proverbs 7:1–3 reminds us that our conscience is strengthened through the study of God's Word.

Help girls to acknowledge that there are absolute truths about sexuality that God has given us. See if they can build a list, which it may be helpful to keep posted in the room and add to as needed. The principles might include the following: Sex is God's idea (Genesis 1:28). Sex is good (Genesis 1:31). Sex is intended for use in a covenant relationship (Genesis 1:24). Sex is more than just a physical act (Matthew 5:27–28). Sex is NOT designed for members within the same family, for same-sex partners, or for humans with animals (Leviticus 18). (Students may be able to think of additional ways in which sinful flesh perverts the divine gift of sexuality.)

Not every sexual issue is black and white. Students have questions about sex not because they haven't been given enough information, but because they experience the tension of conflicting values in our society. You need to be prepared if they ask, "Am I still a virgin if I give or receive oral sex?" "Isn't penetration of the penis into the vagina the proper definition of having sex?" or "God doesn't say it's wrong, so why do I feel guilty?" The following insights may be helpful in answering these types of questions:

Touch is a natural expression of our affection for those around us, and it is possible to touch in ways that are nonsexual yet loving. Certain types of nonsexual touching are a product of time, loyalty, and communication in a relationship, and convey awe and respect for a person.

However, there are actions that cross the line from affection into passionate expression. This line should be guarded with preestablished boundaries, prayer, and a partner who shares similar Christian faith and with whom you share common ideals. But this can be difficult. Girls should know that guys want to be appreciated and have the approval of their partner. Young women want the attention and affection that touch brings. A girl may give sex to feel loved and secure. A guy may say words pledging love and commitment just to get sex. Both are dangerous. Touch can easily be taken too far and become passionate. These passionate touches should be "red flags" for the single person because they were created by God for the sole purpose of leading a married couple to experience the ultimate expression of their covenant relationship—sexual intercourse. It is hard to stop once you progress so far. It is also the nature of sexual sin (and all sin) to want to go farther the next time than you went

before. Each time the boundary moves closer, it will be harder to stop.

On the board or newsprint list the possible negative and positive consequences of making decisions about crossing or not crossing the line of sexual intimacy. (Some possible consequences are listed below.) Have the students focus on the list you prepared. Say, "Every decision you make will have consequences. Decisions about how or when to use your sexuality can negatively or positively affect your body, mind, heart, and spirit. Negative consequences of crossing the line might include STDs, recurring fear of pregnancy, actual pregnancy without the support of a committed spouse, guilt, shame, and damaged relationships in the future. Positive consequences of not crossing the line include healthier relationships, true intimacy, higher self-esteem, and a richer faith."

Discuss the questions that follow with the whole group:

Why do you think God made boundaries for sexual activity? (To show us His plan for intimacy between a man and a woman; so that we might experience true love and intimacy the way He designed them to be.)

How important is it to choose a partner who shares similar values about sex? Why? (It is A LOT more difficult to resist temptation when one or both people are not committed to God's boundaries for sex.)

What activities or suggestions might help or support a couple who wants to "wait"? (Surround themselves with friends who will encourage them and hold them accountable; make definite plans for dates and limit time alone; be strengthened through participation in the Sacraments; confess and received absolution when temptation becomes sin; pray. Other answers may vary.)

For further information, see *The Why Files: When Can I Start Dating? Questions about Love, Sex, and a Cure for Zits* (CPH: 2000).

10 Rotten Reasons—Optional Activity (10 minutes)

Teens hear all kinds of reasons to become sexually active, without learning about any alternatives. Many of these reasons go unchallenged because of the innate sex drive that wants to be satisfied. Peer pressure can make it hard to continue to live in the grace of our Baptism without being ridiculed. It may seem that every other girl in the world but you has had sex. This is not true. This exercise will help girls openly discuss and understand what it is to live as one baptized in Christ.

The list of the "Top 10 Rotten Reasons to Have Sex" is adapted from and explained in greater detail in the book *The Why Files: When Can I Start Dating? Questions about Love, Sex, and a Cure for Zits* (CPH: 2000, pages 160–166). Each student may be provided with her own copy by reproducing Girls Student Page 3B.

Top 10 Rotten Reasons to Have Sex
To Make Love
To Prove Love
To Build Self-Esteem
To Be Socially Accepted
To "Pay" for a Date
To Prove Your Womanhood
To Gain Experience
To Get Pregnant

To Feel Good

To "Just Do It"

Form two groups. Have one group choose one of the "Top 10 Rotten Reasons" and use it to come up with a line that a guy may say to try to persuade a girl to have sex. Let the other group respond with an argument as to why the reason is so rotten.

Closing (2 minutes)

Reaffirm that sexual sin is a serious business that can destroy lives and faith. Strongly affirm that the forgiveness and grace of God will not restore virginity, eliminate a pregnancy, or erase emotional scars, but will sustain a relationship with the heavenly Father and give strength for a life that more closely reflects God's will.

Close this session with the following prayer: "Dear Lord, You are the maker of all good things. You have given us the gift of sexuality. We admit that we have turned this great blessing into something that sometimes brings pain. We know that You desire only the best for our lives. We thank You for Your gracious plan. By Your Spirit help us seek Your will in all that we do, that we may fully experience the goodness of Your gifts. In Jesus' name. Amen."

Paying the Price
Read 1 Corinthians 6:18–20.

Why is sex apart from marriage idolatry?

How is sexual sin different from other sins?

Why do you think this is so?

Do you agree?

What is both exciting and scary about verse 19?

How would you define temple in this context?

Why can we not do whatever we want with our body?

What was the price paid for us?

If you really believe this text, how might you respond?

Top 10 Rotten Reasons to Have Sex

To Make Love

To Prove Love

To Build Self-Esteem

To Be Socially Accepted

To "Pay" for a Date

To Prove Your Womanhood

To Gain Experience

To Get Pregnant

To Feel Good

To "Just Do It"

Adapted from James Watkins, *The Why Files: When Can I Start Dating? Questions about Love, Sex, and a Cure for Zits*
© 2000 Concordia Publishing House.

4 FROM NOW ON

Purpose

No matter what your situation is now, things will continue to change. Our God is the Lord of life and continues to watch over us. We already live in a state of forgiveness through Holy Baptism. You may not be dating now and find this study sort of interesting but irrelevant. Some who have a handle on their sexual behavior now will continue to be tempted and may stray. Some may have already sinned sexually and may wonder if they can be forgiven or if life can be restored. All believers can have confidence that through faith in Jesus, they stand before God as perfectly forgiven by His grace through faith. In Christ we are made new. There is no difference to Him; all who confess Jesus as Lord are redeemed children of God. God can help us move beyond the past and fix our eyes on Christ and the future He has in store for us.

Gospel Emphasis

In John 8:1–11 Jesus does not condemn the woman caught in adultery, but forgives her and calls her to a new commitment to His ways. This is not a license to sin, but God offers us that same gracious forgiveness for our lives.

Lesson Outline

Activity	Time Suggested	Materials Needed
Preparing for a Partner	15 minutes	note cards, markers, pens
A Tale of Two Women	25 minutes	Girls Student Page 4A
Relationship Covenant	10 minutes	Girls Student Page 4B
Six Great Reasons (optional activity)	5 minutes	Girls Student Page 4C
Closing	2 minutes	none

Preparing for a Partner (15 minutes)

It is important for girls to know what they want before they start looking for something. When seeking a husband, girls might want to identify what characteristics for a future partner are important to them. These qualities can be prayed about long before girls meet their future husband. Girls can pray that God would develop these qualities in a future partner and then lead the couple together. More importantly, girls should pray that God would shape them to be the kind of godly wife who would be a great partner in a Christian marriage. Ask the girls to write out on a note card the qualities that they want in their husband. Have girls use the reverse

side of the card to make a list of the characteristics they want to grow in to become the ideal Christian wife. Tell girls to be specific and refer to their lists in the future. Encourage girls to use their list while praying for their own Christian growth and that of their future partner. You may close this activity by praying as a group or in small groups for your students and their future husbands.

A Tale of Two Women (25 minutes)

You may want to divide students into two groups and assign each group one of the lessons to read, answer, and discuss within their group. After allowing time for discussion, have each group take turns sharing their stories, answers, and insights with the other group. Allow time for additional discussion or response during this sharing time. The notes that follow may be used to guide the group discussion.

Read John 4:1–26.

What kinds of things might give someone a bad reputation? (Answers will vary.)

Have you ever had a bad reputation? Why? (Answers will vary.)

How did it affect the relationship between you and your friends, family, or peers? (Answers will vary.)

What are the details about this woman's reputation? (She has had multiple marriages and is now living with someone she's not married to. She is a social and religious outcast in the eyes of the Jews because of her behavior and beliefs. For further details, you may wish to review the notes found in the *Concordia Self-Study Bible* for this section of Scripture.)

Jesus applies the Law by identifying her sin of serial relationships with a lot of men. What do you think is missing in this woman's life that makes her so unsatisfied? (Answers will vary; be sure to include her thirst for true love and intimacy.)

How does Jesus have an answer to her need (thirst)? (He offers complete satisfaction in His Lordship, giving eternal life.)

How might Jesus' words provide relationship satisfaction for you? (When we find satisfaction in Christ, we don't have to chase after cheap substitutes for real love.)

Look at John 8:1–11.

How do the Pharisees (men) react to this woman? (They judge and condemn her.)

How does He apply the Law to this woman? (He tells her to leave her sin.)

How does Jesus apply the Law to her accusers? (He reminds them that they are hypocrites [note that the guilty man is not brought to Jesus], judgmental, and, because they are also sinners, unfit to judge.)

How does He apply the Gospel? (He sends away her accusers, makes the claim of being sinless, and sends her away uncondemned [forgiven] and empowered to live a changed life.)

What do you think Jesus would say to you about your sexuality? (We are forgiven our past sins. He wants us to flee sin in the future and empowers us to live for Him.)

What can you learn about God's will for your sexuality from these two stories? (Answers will vary. Focus on the satisfaction found in Christ, the

forgiveness offered by Him, and the strength God gives to lead a changed life.)

Relationship Covenant (10 minutes)

As you make a transition into a closing for this study, say, "God in His grace says that we can love because He first loved us. Christ's giving, serving, selfless love changes us to be like Him. It also guides our actions and decisions, as He gives us patience to wait for His blessing, and strength to resist temptation in the meantime. Our lives are a reflection of what Christ has worked in our Baptism. Our sexuality is as powerful as it is unique. The power of the Holy Spirit helps us to guard against going outside of God's desire for how we use this gift. Through a faith relationship with God, as His Spirit continues to work in our lives, sin no longer has control over us."

This activity is designed to remind students that it is only with the power of God that we can overcome temptation in our lives; without Him we are helpless. Distribute copies of Girls Student Page 4B. Say, "This covenant is a reminder of the covenant that God established with us in our Baptism to make us His daughters. Throughout the Bible and in Holy Communion, He reminds us of this relationship that He established with us and empowers us to have healthier relationships with those around us." Encourage students to pray silently for God to guide their use of His gift of sexuality, and then complete and sign the covenant form.

Six Great Reasons—Optional Activity (5 minutes)

The list of "Six Great Reasons to Have Sex" is taken from and explained in greater detail in the book *The Why Files: When Can I Start Dating? Questions about Love, Sex, and a Cure for Zits* (CPH: 2000, pp. 166–71). Reproduce Girls Student Page 4C so that each student may receive her own copy. Use the list as a discussion starter with the students. Invite them to post this reminder at home. Ask how each of the statements can affect their lives.

Six Great Reasons to Have Sex
To Express Love as Christ Has for His Bride, the Church
To Express a Lifelong Commitment
To Express a Lifelong Love
To Give and Receive Pleasure
To Grow Closer Together Mentally, Emotionally, and Spiritually
To Bring New Life into the World

Use this list as a discussion starter with the students. How can each of the statements affect their lives?

Closing (2 minutes)

Close this session with the following prayer: "Most loving Father, Your grace is beyond our imagination. You have shown Your love to all people through the work of Your Son. Please forgive us for the times we have strayed outside of Your will for our lives. We admit that our way is wrong and Your way is right. Thank You for desiring to offer grace and every blessing to each and every one of us, and for giving us Your Word to

reveal yourself and draw us closer to You. Thank You for the forgiveness You freely offer to us. We ask that You would be truly present in and strengthen our relationships. Remind us daily of Your incredible relationship with us. Through Jesus Christ we pray. Amen."

A Tale of Two Women
Read John 4:1–26.

What kinds of things might give someone a bad reputation?

Have you ever had a bad reputation? Why?

How did it affect the relationship between you and your friends, family, or peers?

What are the details about this woman's reputation?

Jesus applies the Law by identifying her sin of serial relationships with a lot of men. What do you think is missing in this woman's life that makes her so unsatisfied?

How does Jesus offer an answer to her need (thirst)?

How might Jesus' words provide relationship satisfaction for you?

Look at John 8:1–11.

How do the Pharisees (men) react to this woman?

How does Jesus apply the Law to this woman? How does He apply the Law to her accusers?

How does He apply the Gospel?

What do you think Jesus would say to you about your sexuality?

What can you learn about God's will for your sexuality from these two stories?

I, _____, realize that my body is

not my own. I was bought with a price. At my Baptism God placed

His name upon my heart and made me His child. He wants what is

best for me and desires that all my actions, words, and even my

thoughts be pleasing in His sight. He is the perfect, loving Father and He

forgives me, no matter what I have done. I know that what is past is forgiv-

en through God's graceful act of faith in Christ, and God has given me a

clean slate, a new beginning each day. With this covenant I remember the

relationship that God has established with me, and I ask God to help me

never to replace that bond with any guy here on earth. I acknowledge that it

is most important that God's relationship with me come before all others.

With God's help I will honor the body He has given me for His glory.

Signed _____ Date _____

Six Great Reasons to Have Sex

To Express Love as Christ Has for His Bride, the Church

To Express a Lifelong Commitment

To Express a Lifelong Love

To Give and Receive Pleasure

To Grow Closer Together Mentally, Emotionally, and Spiritually

To Bring New Life into the World

Excerpted from James Watkins, *The Why Files: When Can I Start Dating? Questions about Love, Sex, and a Cure for Zits* © 2000 Concordia Publishing House.

Additional Resources

Additional materials for use with *Girl Stuff: Dating and Sexuality* are available from Concordia Publishing House at no additional charge. Simply visit the CPH Web site at www.cph.org/youth/guygirl/dating.